"The aim of marketing is to know and understand the customer so well the product or service sells itself."

Peter Drucker

The Marketing Audit

The hidden link between customer engagement and sustainable revenue growth

THIS BOOK CONTAINS A 50 QUESTION CHECKLIST TO GET YOU STARTED ON PERFORMING A MARKETING AUDIT FOR YOUR COMPANY. IF YOU DON'T KNOW THE ANSWERS TO THESE QUESTIONS, YOU ARE LOSING OPPORTUNITIES AND CUSTOMERS!

Knowledge Insights for Business Success

Orlando Skelton, MBA

A Guide to Performing a Marketing Audit: A Case Study

ISBN: 978-1-329-19051-1

The names, characters, businesses, organizations, places, events and incidents used in this book either are the product of the author's experience or used fictitiously to protect the identity of the participants. Any resemblance to actual persons, living or dead, events, or locales is entirely coincidental.

For questions, comments, or to be a guest on our weekly radio show contact us at:

SCH Consulting
228 Park Avenue S, Suite 20725
New York, NY 10003
consulting@schmc.com
Twitter: SCH360

Scan this code or go to http://delivr.com/2jw6g to register for a free bonus book.

This book is dedicated to the members of our research team and staff who diligently and enthusiastically support our community of small business owners, entrepreneurs, partners, and students.

Contents

"The aim of marketing is to know and understand the customer so well the product or service sells itself."

Peter Drucker

Marketing in the 21st century has become a challenging endeavor for small business owners. One thought leader described the new environment as follows, "There is an enormous evolution in the world of marketing as traditional forms of media are decreasing in effectiveness and are being replaced by new media." Additionally, in a recent survey by a team of researchers, two-thirds of survey respondents felt they were overwhelmed by advertising that had little or no relevance to their daily activities. At the same time, the introduction of new technologies such as digital video recorders, video-on-demand, and online webcasting has allowed consumers the ability to bypass advertising messages based upon their personal preferences.

Today, consumers can access real-time information about performance and customer satisfaction ratings of products/services of any company via blogs, chat rooms, user generated content or direct feedback from purchasers. The growth of the Internet has given birth to a new class of consumer who values convenience, instant gratification, access to information, and products customized or personalized to their needs. As consumer preferences continue to evolve, small business owners will also face challenges in defining metrics to determine the success of their marketing efforts and measure return on investment in this new environment.

Because of these challenges, small business owners must continue to innovate to deliver its message to target audiences. On balance, the application of new media technologies enables expanded opportunities for small business owners to develop new business models and build stronger relationships with customers. This book presents information on how small business owners, entrepreneurs, and marketing professionals can perform a marketing audit to improve customer engagement and business performance.

Personalization

Small business owners are seeking to use personalization as a method of increasing the return on their marketing investments. The main challenge of personalization, from a marketing viewpoint, is the lack of a common framework through which consumers and small business owners can communicate. Researchers identified seven different interpretations of communication frameworks, which compared and contrasted the differences between personalization and customization.

Our view of personalization falls between the definition where personalization is a specialized form of product differentiation tailored to a particular individual and the meaning where personalization has to be initiated by the customer. For example, car dealers have cars available on the property from which consumers can choose to purchase. In such cases, the car may not have the exact features desired, but fall within the range of acceptability for the customer to complete the transaction. The selection of features available in the dealer's on-site inventory is typically the result of marketing research performed by the dealer or the automobile manufacturer. Alternatively, if the dealer's on-site inventory does not match the wants and needs of the consumer, a vehicle can be ordered directly from the factory to their exact specifications. Thus personalization, in the authors' view, cannot be accomplished without the active participation of the consumer.

The benefit of personalized marketing for companies is the ability to charge higher prices, increase customer loyalty, and improve customer satisfaction. However; companies should only undertake personalization if the costs, which may require investments in technology, consumer education, and branding yields an acceptable return (tangible and intangible) on such investments. In field experiments, we found that hand-written, personalized notes increased requests for samples indicating personalization has a positive consumer response.

Researcher's Peppers, Rogers, and Dorf[1], outlined a process by which companies can implement a personalized marketing program. They suggested that companies should undertake steps to identify customers, differentiate between them, find opportunities to interact, and then finally customize their products or services to meet customer needs. While this approach may appear straightforward, it is very

---

[1] Is your company ready for one to one marketing, Harvard Business Review.

difficult to implement in practice due to logistical and coordination challenges. Personalized marketing, when correctly implemented, can pay dividends in strengthening relationships with customers.

Dynamic Pricing

One of the goals of personalized or one-to-one marketing is to connect on a deeper level with customers resulting in stronger customer loyalty and the opportunity to charge premium prices for their products and services. For example, Caterpillar uses a layered approach to communicating its perceived value to customers by identifying characteristics such as superior service, durability, reliability, and offering a longer warranty. Managerial research revealed that there is growing evidence to indicate dynamic pricing offers a tempting opportunity to increase profitability. Researchers also note there is significant potential for trust deterioration between the company and the customer if it becomes known the company engages in dynamic pricing practices whereby the same class of customer are charged different prices. For example, consumers are more tolerant of price differences for seniors, students, or clients in various geographic regions, but react negatively if price differences are perceived to be based on demand or not related to increased costs.

Further, researchers identified three pricing models used primarily in retail stores. The first-degree pricing model focuses on price-conscious consumers. The second level competed directly with national brands and priced approximately 20% lower than the equivalent national brands. The final pricing model targets quality conscious customers.

Marketing experts Kotler and Keller noted; a product can be priced using a variety of methods such as a simple markup, perceived value, the rate of return, or auction. Each approach has its advantages and disadvantages. First-degree price discrimination is the most profitable because it has the potential to capture the full value of the product or service being offered. However, second-degree price discrimination consists of offering a variety of pricing options that allow the user to choose the desired pricing option based on individual wants, needs, or financial capabilities. This approach is an approach where personalization is a form of product differentiation and that consumers must participate in the personalization process as it relates to pricing policies to maintain consumer trust.

Key Insights

The key finding of our research revealed

1. Small business owners must personalize their marketing messages to navigate successfully through the tremendous amount of advertising background noise. Small business owners must undertake steps to identify customers, differentiate between them, find opportunities to interact, and finally customize its products or services to meet customer needs.

2. Second, marketing professionals should continue to innovate and develop new business models utilizing new media technologies. Successful companies will utilize blogs, video-on-demand,

webcasting, websites, and other multifunctional devices to their advantage as consumers gain greater control over how, when, and where they consume information.

3. Third, it is a necessity for companies to invest in and harmonize customers online and off-line experiences as part of a multichannel strategy. Consumers will demand the ability to order online and retrieve/return the product at the supplier storefronts or other distribution point, as well as navigate seamlessly between the two domains.

4. Fourth, as domestic industries approach maturity; global expansion will provide access to new markets and revenue growth opportunities. The evidence of globalization is visible everywhere as companies face competitors in their home markets as well as competitors from abroad. Marketing managers will have to compete with new global competitors requiring innovative and aggressive responses including collaborating with other firms and intermediaries to enhance their competitive capabilities.

5. Finally, the critical success factor that connects marketing theory to practice/application whether, in the creation, manufacture, execution or provision of products (services) to customers is the "people" component. Essentially, this means having the right people in the right positions, with the right skills.

Often, information contained in application or practitioner-oriented books such as this one can be difficult to interpret and apply in the business setting of the reader. To simplify the problem of transitioning from theory to application, we provide a roadmap (case study) to illustrate how performing a marketing audit can uncover hidden links between customer expectations and sustainable long-term revenue growth.

The next section presents an actual Case Study to illustrate how to perform a marketing audit to uncover problems and knowledge, customer expectation, and capability gaps. The findings from the marketing audit will provide business leaders and entrepreneurs with actionable insights to improve the effectiveness of their marketing activities and initiatives.

Case Study

The information contained in this case study used data collected and analyzed from a service-based satellite communications company. ASC (fictitious name) started as a "mom and pop" business 27 years ago by a sales manager in the emerging commercial satellite communications industry. The commercialization of space was spurred on by the then famous launch of the Russian satellite, Sputnik. Today, satellites positioned over the world are providing services such as television programming distribution, telephone communications, radio, global positioning, weather reporting, and data networking.

ASC is in the business of remarketing and reselling excess inventory from satellite operators and third party end users. ASC customers engage in activities related to newsgathering, sporting event production, entertainment program syndication, evangelical religious programming, education/learning, subscriber-based/pay television network services, and cable television distribution. The company has 22 employees and revenues of approximately $23M.

The consolidation of the satellite industry, predatory pricing by competitors, customer price sensitivity, and flat annual revenues caused ASC management to reevaluate its business plan. The purpose of this consulting engagement was to identify areas where ASC could improve its marketing performance thru a comprehensive review of the company's marketing strategies, objectives, and marketplace activities. The Marketing Audit included an assessment of the macro-environment, a task audit, the internal marketing organization, evaluating the ASC's marketing strategy, and analyzing overall business performance. Interviews with the Chief Executive Officer, the Vice President of Finance, the Manager of Operations, and members of the sales staff were the primary sources of data collection for the marketing audit. The audit of the marketing function should also include customer feedback.

The Environment

Marketing is contest for people's attention.

Seth Godin

The macro-environment audit provides management with insights into the essential industry demographic, economic, technological, regulatory, and cultural trends. The information received from this section of the marketing audit will allow management to position (or re-position) the company's services in the marketplace.

Industry Demographics

Statistics published by the Satellite Industry Association, revenue growth in the global satellite industry including satellite launch vehicle providers and manufacturers, increased to $144.4 billion or 19% at the time of the marketing audit[2]. Globally, satellites are used to transmit television signals to homes, gather and distribute news, connect mobile devices such as telephones, and transport data. Revenue growth in the satellite industry results from technological innovation, the increasing use of information technology services by businesses, and consumer spending. Individual company profitability depends upon efficient operations and good marketing. The primary growth segment of the satellite industry is the provision of satellite services

---

[2] Data obtained from the Satellite Industry Association.

similar to those offered by ASC. The Chief Executive Officer (CEO) of the world's largest satellite operator, David McGlade, commented that the best customer market segments were network services, media, and government. Over the past decade, there has been a consolidation of domestic satellite operators from five to three. Industry consolidation is a significant threat to ASC because as competition intensifies for each sales opportunity profit margins decline making it more difficult for ASC to compete against satellite operators.

Economic

The satellite industry is growing despite the global recession. Historically, economic downturns have had a delayed effect on the satellite industry, according to the Satellite Industry Association. The industry is also experiencing rising satellite launch and construction costs due to fluctuating currency exchange rates.

Satellite insurance premiums are at risk because of in-orbit satellite component failures. Difficulties experienced in the financial markets has significantly impacted the ability to raise capital in the satellite industry for the investment in plant, machinery, and infrastructure maintenance. Telecommunications companies make annual capital investments up to 20 percent of revenue resulting in high debt levels, exposing them to interest rate change risks.

Technological

New technologies and applications such as High Definition (HD) and 3D video, mobile voice/data services for automobiles, trains, and airplanes will be growth drivers for the telecommunications industry. However, the satellite industry faces competitive threats from alternative technologies such as Wi-Fi, WiMax, fiber, more efficient data compression algorithms, and signal modulation techniques. Also, new competitors are entering the market such as telephone companies and cable television companies. These companies are expanding their product lines to add internet connectivity and telephone services.

Political/Regulatory

The Federal Communications Commission (FCC) regulates the satellite industry. The FCC issues licenses for the construction, launch, and operation of satellites in the United States and coordinates telecommunications policy with the International Telecommunications Union (ITU). The operations, cost and licensing of radio frequency spectrum, the right to transmit and receive satellites signals, and in some cases pricing, is regulated or strongly influenced by local, state, and federal agencies. Other key industry regulatory organizations include the Telecommunications Industry Association (TIA), the National Telecommunications Infrastructure Association (NTIA), and the United States Telecom Association (USTelecom).

Cultural

The satellite industry is not influenced by cultural factors such as lifestyle, customs, religion, or traditions.

Task Audit

Marketing is too important to be left exclusively to the marketing department.

David Packard

The purpose of the task environment audit is to develop a deeper understanding of the forces that are directly linked to the production, distribution, and promotion of a company's products and services.

Markets

The Satellite Industry is a niche part of the Telecommunications Industry. In the United States, there are approximately 11,000 companies that provide telecommunication services generating annual revenues of approximately $500 billion. The major market segments are wireline carriers, wireless companies, cable companies, satellite companies, and telecommunication resellers. The telecom industry has a high level of concentration with the 50 largest companies controlling approximately 90% of the market. The satellite industry sub-segment (which includes satellite companies, cable television providers, and telecommunications resellers), includes 1,400 companies with total annual revenues of $100 billion.

Customers

According to Jiang and Tuzhilin[3], intelligent customer segmentation is critical for companies to deliver personalized and targeted products and services to its customers. As stated in the introduction, ASC clients are engaged in the business of newsgathering, sports production services, entertainment program syndicators, religious organizations, educational institutions, subscriber-based/pay television networks, and cable television companies. Due to the diversity of ASC's customer base, the management has segmented its customer base by needs and buying process.

The first customer segment is "Wholesale" (also known as "in-house" inventory). In the wholesale segment, ASC buys inventory from the satellite operators on a long-term basis to fix its inventory and to provide protection against future price increases. ASC purchases its inventory from all satellite operators in the industry to ensure good relationships with suppliers and to offer the widest range of services possible to customers.

The wholesale sales channel is the most profitable customer segment for the company and requires the largest financial commitment by ASC. Customers in this segment make their buying decisions based on price and long-term assurance of inventory availability. As a result, customers in this segment enter into multi-year contractual agreements.

---

[3] Dynamic micro-targeting: Fitness-based approach to predicting individual preferences, Knowledge and Information Systems. See Additional Reading section.

The second customer segment is "Revenue-Share." In this customer segment, ASC contracts with customers who have purchased capacity directly from the satellite operator (secondary market). These customers have excess inventory because of changes in their business plan, implementation of more efficient technology, or loss of business. However, because they entered into long-term contracts with the satellite operators, they must keep the contracted satellite capacity for the duration of their contracts. ASC contracts with these customers on a revenue share basis to augment their inventory, increase revenue potential, and help customers offset fixed costs. Customers in this segment make their buying decisions based upon which reseller can generate the most revenue to offset their fixed costs. The relationship with the reseller, past performance, and service quality are key decision factors in the selection of a partner. Customer contracts in this segment are typically month-to-month. Therefore, customer satisfaction and performance is critical.

The third customer segment is "Ad-Hoc/Third Party." ASC places customers in this segment when it does not have any "in-house" or "revenue share" inventory available due to prior sales. This source of inventory is idle (unsold) satellite capacity offered for sale by the satellite operator, on a short-term basis (for example, hourly, daily, or weekly only). In this customer segment, ASC will perform various customer service activities and invoice the customer for services provided. The main challenge in supporting this customer segment is the variability of available inventory and cost, which is dependent upon market supply and demand characteristics. This segment is highly competitive due to the short-term nature of inventory availability where price and response time are the key drivers.

The company performed its last customer survey over three years ago using in-house resources. The customer survey did not contain any questions comparing ASC to the competition on service quality, reputation, its sales force, or pricing policies. As noted, feedback from customer surveys (formally and informally is a critical component of the marketing audit.[4]

Competitors

The CEO noted; ASC has two main competitors. Starlight (fictitious name) is the smallest competitor of the two competitors. Starlight's revenues are one-fifth of ASC's, and their market strategy was based upon the long-term personal industry relationships of the sole business owner. Starlight competes directly with ASC in the ad-hoc/third-party customer segment. Starlight is the only remaining small satellite capacity reseller independently owned by the founder and not funded by a major reseller or satellite operator.

The second competitor and largest integrated reseller is Satcom America, Inc. (Satcom). Satcom (fictitious name) provides end-to-end satellite and terrestrial solutions to its customers. While ASC could offer services similar to Satcom through partnerships with terrestrial service providers, it would be difficult for ASC to maintain end-to-end service

---

[4] Review our publication library for information on how to perform a customer survey.

quality and directly control the user experience of their customers.

Satcom is significantly larger than ASC with over 800 employees. Satcom and is owned by a European telecommunications company, which provides satellite and other telecommunication based services to over 14 countries. All firms in the marketplace occupied by ASC, Starlight, and Satcom are affected by the introduction and evolution of wireless technologies. In addition, expansion of fiber deployment to business and residential customers are potential substitutes for the distribution of video programming via satellite.

Distribution and Dealers

ASC is part of a distributed value chain, and as such does not provide service directly to the customer. Customers typically call the ASC operations center to schedule satellite time to transmit their programming. At the scheduled time, the customer will call the satellite operator's Access Center to begin transmitting to the satellite.

Upon the conclusion of the service, ASC will bill the customer for the satellite time used and subsequently pay the satellite operator less their profit margin. New scheduling systems are being introduced into the marketplace that can electronically link customers to ASC's databases to query and potentially purchase services without the need for telephone calls or human intervention.

Suppliers

As noted earlier, the suppliers of satellite capacity to ASC are the owners of satellites and secondarily customers who have purchased capacity directly from satellites owners. Over the past few years, there has been a consolidation of domestic satellite operators serving North America. Further consolidation in the domestic market, although not likely due to the high level of market control by the world's first and second largest satellite operators, is a significant threat to resellers.

Facilitators and Marketing Firms

ASC does not utilize the services of marketing research reports to track customer or market trends. However, there are marketing research companies that specialize in the satellite industry and publish industry reports. According to the CEO, further research is needed to determine costs, benefits, and effectiveness of expenditures in this area.

Marketing Audit

Brands are faced with the daily challenge of massively scaling their outreach in order to build personal relationships. While this may seem like a contradiction in terms, it becomes much more possible when brands shift from push to pull dynamics in their marketing.

Simon Mainwaring

Researcher's Chambers, Kouvelis, and Semple[5] noted that consumers have numerous opportunities to interact with the providers of competing products and services and must make a vendor selection based upon their perception of quality and price. The Marketing Function Audit provides a comprehensive analysis of the company's products/services, pricing strategies, distribution channels, advertising, promotion, and strategic objectives.

Products/Services

ASC offers three services targeted to different customer needs and buying processes. The company does not have a formal marketing plan nor has it established any specific goals or objectives for each customer segment.

---

[5] Quality-based competition, profitability, and variable costs, Management Science.

Price

The CEO commented they establish pricing based on what the company refers to as "rate cards." Rate cards are built depending upon the source of the inventory (satellite operator, third party, or internal), market conditions, annual revenue generated by the customer, and the competition for a particular opportunity. Rate cards are updated periodically as market conditions change.

The company utilizes an automated scheduling system that contains a large amount of historical marketing information on the type of services rendered, price, and purchase frequency. Efficient data mining of this information will allow the company to establish pricing strategies and internal procedures to maximize profitability. Also, the analysis of the data obtained from the customer survey, coupled with the data contained in the scheduling database will provide ASC with a deeper understanding of its customers resulting in actionable business insights.

Distribution

ASC's sales force has three direct sales managers and five agents who offer services to the marketplace on behalf of the company. These individuals leverage their personal relationships and extended professional networks to educate existing and potential customers about the services offered by ASC. In recent months, the company has added independent sales agents as a strategy or for expanding market coverage without significantly increasing personnel costs.

Integrated Marketing Communications

Advertising is not a high priority for ASC. Researchers Berthon, Ewing, and Napoli[6] explained that the management style of Small to Medium Enterprises (SME's) are different from larger organizations due to limited resources. Only recently, for the first time in the history of the company, ASC exhibited at a trade show and advertised in industry trade magazines. According to the CEO, ASC is the industry's best kept secret.

The main source of advertising for ASC is the satellite inventory report sent to customers on a monthly basis. ASC does not use online marketing, sales promotions, or other forms of advertising/marketing due to a lack of internal marketing expertise and limited financial resources. SME's often have time and financial resource constraints, which results in managers adopting a survival mentality. Inadequate strategic planning compounds this problem.

Marketing Strategy Audit

Taghian and Shaw[7] noted marketing strategy requires a dual focus on both customers and competitors. Marketing includes (1) collection of market intelligence on present and potential customers and competitors, (2) managing

---

[6] Brand management in small to medium-sized enterprises, Journal of Small Business Management.

[7] The marketing audit and organizational performance: An empirical profiling, Journal of Marketing Theory and Practice.

information to develop market knowledge, and (3) the capability to respond to market dynamics when opportunities or threats arise. The Marketing Strategy Audit provides a systematic, orderly examination of a company's strategic marketing objectives with the goal of improving profitability, and performance of marketing initiatives. As noted by Berthon et al., SME managers are often the sole decision-maker and handle functions within the organization such as banking, advertising, and recruitment. The use of specialists is usually very rare. Although, the management aspires to develop a marketing strategy, ASC's current approach to marketing is primarily through its sales team.

Business Mission

ASC did not have a formal written Mission Statement.

Marketing Objectives and Goals

As noted earlier, the company does not have a formal marketing plan. However, ASC has identified several marketing projects such as the redesign of its website, the engagement of marketing expertise on a project-by-project basis, and introducing targeted sales promotions. The CEO makes all marketing decisions at ASC, and the company does not employ marketing personnel or contract with third parties for marketing, advertising, or public relation services.

According to Kotler and Keller[8], brand equity is the essence of what differentiates a product from the competition. Using the Brand Asset Valuator Model (Figure 1.), which

---

[8] Marketing Management, Pearson Education.

consists of five brand elements (differentiation, energy, relevance, esteem, and knowledge), ASC is positioned in the quadrant that represents low brand stature and low energized brand strength resulting in an unfocused brand development/management approach.

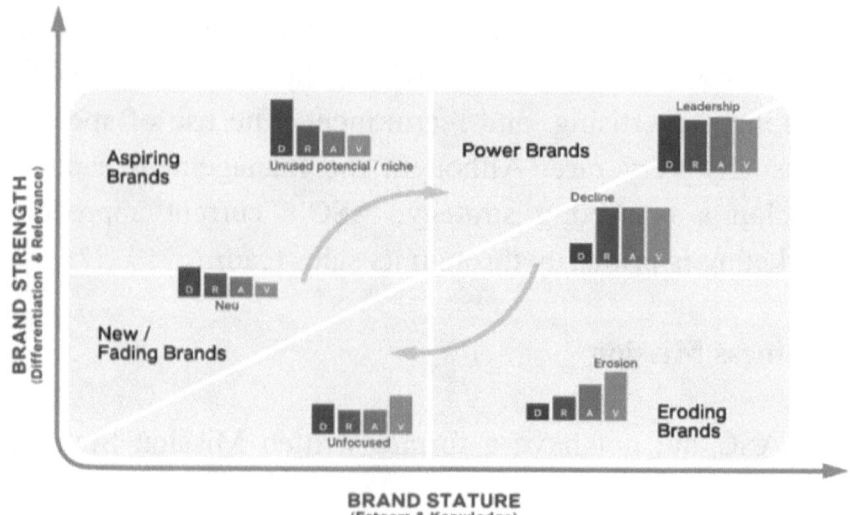

Figure 1. The brand bubble: The looming crisis in brand value and how to avoid it by J. Gerzema and E. Lebar. Copyright 2008 by Jossey-Bass. Reproduced with permission.

Performance Metrics

The company uses and tracks a limited set of performance metrics (Revenue, Inventory Utilization) on a monthly basis and does not have a formal marketing strategy at this time. The management has acknowledged because of the Marketing Audit interview process, more focus on its marketing function is needed as well as establishing and tracking a broader set of performance metrics (i.e., scorecards).

Recommendations

The purpose of this case study was to identify areas where ASC can improve its marketing performance through a comprehensive audit of the company's marketing strategies, objectives, and marketplace activities. The results of this comprehensive Marketing Audit indicate several areas for improvement. First, the company should conduct a customer survey. The key steps for conducting a successful customer survey are:

(a) establish clear and quantifiable objectives,

(b) involve senior management,

(c) include customer perspectives,

(d) encourage a high level of customer participation,

(e) develop action plans and timelines,

(f) communicate the results to customers/employees, and

(g) make the review process continuous to ensure customer alignment with marketing goals (Katcher)[9].

Second, the company must strengthen its internal marketing expertise through recruiting new employees with the required skills or outsource key marketing functions to third parties, as resources permit. Finally, the CEO must

---

[9] Make more strategic use of customer satisfaction surveys, The Journal of Business Strategy.

develop, promote, and establish a marketing/brand vision for the company. This action starts with a business mission statement, setting measurable marketing objectives and preparing a formal marketing plan to build the company's brand.

People are in such a hurry to launch their product or business that they seldom look at marketing from a bird's eye view and they don't create a systematic plan.

Dave Ramsey

Berthon, P., Ewing, M. T., & Napoli, J. Brand management in small to medium-sized enterprises. Journal of Small Business Management, *46*(1), 27-45. doi:10.1111/j.1540-627X.2007.00229.x

Chambers, C., Kouvelis, P., & Semple. J. Quality-based competition, profitability, and variable costs. Management Science, *52*, 1884 1895. doi:10.1287/mnsc.1060.0581

Goldsmith, R. E. Current and future trends in marketing and their implications for the discipline. *Journal of Marketing Theory and Practice, 12*(4), 10-17.

Haag, S., & Cummings, M. Management information systems for the information age (Laureate Education, Inc.). Boston: McGraw-Hill/Irwin.

Halliday, S., Badenhorst, K., & Solms, R. A business approach to effective information technology risk analysis and management. Information Management &

Computer Security, *4*(1). Retrieved from ABI/INFORM Global database.

Howard, D. J., & Kerin, R. A. The effects of personalized product recommendations on advertisement response rates: The "Try this. It works! technique. *Journal of Consumer Psychology, 14*(3), 271-279. doi:10.1207/s15327663jcp1403_8

Jiang, T., & Tuzhilin, A. Dynamic micro-targeting: fitness-based approach to predicting individual preferences. Knowledge and Information Systems, *19*, 337-360. doi:10.1007/s10115-008-0149-z

Katcher, B. Make more strategic use of customer satisfaction surveys. The Journal of Business Strategy, *24*(1), 34-37. doi:10.1108/02756660310734893

Kotler, P., & Keller, K. L. Marketing management. Upper Saddle River, New Jersey: Pearson Education's, Inc.

Mohamed, M., Stankosky, M., & Murray, A. Knowledge management and information technology: can they work in perfect harmony? Journal of Knowledge Management, *10*, 103-116. doi:10.1108/13673270610670885

Peppers, D., Rodgers, M., & Dorf, B. Is your company ready for one to one marketing? *Harvard Business Review, 77*(1), 151-160.

Prahalad, C., & Ramaswamy, V. Co-creation
experiences: The next practice in value creation.
Journal of Interactive Marketing, 5-14.
doi:10.1002/dir.20015

Taghian, M., & Shaw, R. The marketing audit and
organizational performance: An empirical
profiling. Journal of Marketing Theory and
Practice, *16*, 341-350. doi:10.2753/MTP1069-
6679160406

Note: If you cannot get access to these articles, send us an
email and we will help you retrieve them.

This checklist is a starting point to begin auditing the marketing function in your company. The person responsible for conducting the marketing audit should interview key members of the organization in leadership, finance, marketing, sales, and customer service using the questions listed below to capture different perspectives and to determine the strategic alignment (or misalignment) of the marketing function. As a purchaser of this book, you are entitled to a one-on-one session to help you get started. We can be contacted via our email address (shown at the beginning of this book) or through our website (www.schmc.com).

- What major opportunities (or threats) do you see for your company this year?

- Are you planning to introduce any new services? What problem will the new services(s) solve for the customer?

- Do you have any evidence/research/data to support the launch of this service? Did the customer help you design the new service?

- What external forces or trends do you see that will have an impact on your marketing strategy or success of the company?

- How is your marketing function organized? Do you have adequate resources and staff trained in marketing?

- How do your customers feel about the company's services?

- Do you routinely survey your customers? If so, how frequently? If not, why?

- What were the major findings from the survey? Who are your major competitors? Do you have an action plan and a lead person to follow-up (quickly) all issues uncovered in the survey?

- What trends are occurring among the market leading suppliers in your industry?

- How effective are the company's advertising agencies and marketing research firms? If you do not use the services of these firms, how do you capture market trends and customer buying habits?

- What are the company's product line objectives?

- What areas of product and brand strategy need improvement? Do you have plans in place to address deficiencies?

- What are the company's pricing objectives, policies, strategies, and procedures? How frequently are they reviewed?

- Is there adequate market trade/press coverage for your services?

- How would you rate the market awareness of your company and its services?

- What are the organization's advertising objectives?

- What advertising vehicles do you use? How effective are they? Do you use A/B split testing?

- Is there effective and sufficient use of sales promotion tools such as samples, coupons, displays, and sales contests?

- Is the business mission clearly stated in market-oriented terms?

- Are the company's marketing goals and objectives stated clearly enough to guide market planning and performance measurement?

- What are the pricing trends for your services (and competitors) over the past year? How will this trend affect your company, suppliers, and customers?

- What is the growth potential for each customer segment?

- How is the company's performing (metrics) with respect to the delivery of services?

- What tools do you use to measure the non-financial aspects of your business (i.e., customer loyalty and retention, market share, service delivery cycle time, customer complaints, and time to resolution)?

- What are your customer segments? How do you segment them and why? How often do you review customer segmentation and segment profitability?

- How do customers rate the company and its competitors on reputation, quality, and price?

- How do customers in different segments make their buying decisions? What are their objectives, strategies, strengths, weaknesses, and sizes?

- How do you attract new customers? Which sales channels are more effective for lead generation? Do you track how many new customers or prospects contact you daily? How do you capture this information?

- What is the growth potential for each customer segment?

- How does the company offer its services?

- Do you capture metrics from your website? How many new leads do you receive from your website on a daily, weekly, or monthly basis? How effectively is your website in generating leads?

- How are revenue goals established? Is there a formalized process?

- Do you use benchmarking tools to evaluate the performance of your business? Are you maximizing the value of your business?

- Have you have your business evaluated to determine the value (i.e., selling price)? I s the value of your business increasing or decreasing?

About the Author

Orlando Skelton is the Managing Director of SCH Consulting and Chief Technology Officer of The eLearning Center. Mr. Skelton has extensive professional experience in Sales, Marketing, Business Development, and Technical Customer Service. Mr. Skelton is a recipient of numerous awards for his leadership skills, creativity, and ability to assemble high-performing teams. In addition, Mr. Skelton performed as a Chapter 11 and Chapter 7 Bankruptcy Trustee managing distressed media and telecommunication companies.

Mr. Skelton is passionate about entrepreneurship and hosts *Knowledge Insights for Business Success*; a weekly radio show focused on helping business owners and entrepreneurs to build strong customer relationships, create better products, use performance analytics to manage their business, and help them to develop cost-effective revenue growth strategies. Also to his consulting, writing, and mentoring activities, Mr. Skelton participates in microfinance loan programs that support entrepreneurs in third-world countries to help improve the quality of life for them and their families.

Mr. Skelton holds degrees in Electrical Engineering from the University of Evansville and an MBA from the University of California. Mr. Skelton completed post-graduate work at Walden University in the areas of Information Technology & Knowledge Management. He also completed the Investment Banking program at New York University and currently trains students globally in Marketing, Finance, Accounting, and Management through eLearning programs.

www.ingramcontent.com/pod-product-compliance
Lightning Source LLC
Chambersburg PA
CBHW021850170526
45157CB00006B/2389